VIOLENCE

Lauren Crowley

First paperback edition published in 2017 by Crowley Press
LaurenCorinneCrowley.com

Printed in the United States of America

Library of Congress Cataloging-in-Publication Data
ISBN: 978-0-9982322-3-2
1. Poetry 2. Women writers

To my animus

Part I

(Picture in an encyclopedia)

I have a GARGANTUAN body,
in which there are little holes where little birds live,
make love, learn to court, for so many centuries they
have learned to do this, and each of them cried when
a feather was plucked out, because loving becomes
rough when the birds forget themselves,

and at some point the birds must migrate,
leave the holes to go back, and most of them
get lost, while the others somewhere die. the holes
are left to close up, the body enclosed by lines

and when it lies next to a body without holes,
the memory of birds singing seems to float,
and I don't think I could hold a single tear
back, they are holes unto themselves

(I've been a hole unto myself, and so
nothing does as nothing is, it
floats and floats and floats)

April 23, 2017

(I think they were orange, I know they were bright)

It was rumored once that I was filled with fireflies and my secret smile said it was true but then-

a storm blew in and every light wore a coat of fog and it went on like this for so long that I, too, thought it a rumor

it went on for so long that I became water

Enough time passed and we could create fireflies in labs,

I tried to describe the shape, the sound, the scent of mine

they gave me four holograms and a receipt but it wasn't quite the same,

because even when we draw our dreams in crayon or in pencil they
do not look the same, I do not look the same, discord stole my smile
like a thief in the night

April 23, 2017

(There's no fire undersea)

And so I moved to the bottom of the ocean where Neptune ate and drank,
I pretended to be his daughter and suffocated each night, water is no food,
blue had hands to choke me, and I was too slim to stomach the moon,

Imagine lighting a match down there, it just won't strike

April 23, 2017

(Moment or montage)

Because I saw myself as a princess I became one,
and every window is my pyre, and every moment,
I am beneath the fire, it is true I have felt like a
nothing, camouflaged by a kaleidoscope whose
batteries have run dry, some other things are
true, but I have not felt them, and I've been
told I can create anything from a thought,
and so I became afraid of my mind, I am
the only actor in a documentary, playing
the role of a woman I never met, all I have
is the script, but the director says: 'why don't
you improvise?' like I am a director, too. at least
the costume's real, at least my makeup is done well,
you can win awards for that, you know. and I'm gunning
for gold.

April 26, 2017

(Mutation)

I think there is a moment far away, where the earth takes pity on me,
and washes my dead arms away in the stream, mangled and purple
and grey like spoilt meat. I'm ripping apart the devil-sewn seams,
proclaiming myself armless, so something true will grow back,
hands that hold you like an angel, I want only to bless you,
I am nailless and toothless and even my stomach will be gutted,
too, I want to scoop out all the rot that confuses you, see, sometimes
a tree grows a limb, maybe two, that god did not design and the soul
cannot approve, and I'm cutting them all off, this I promise to you,
there's a me I can remember, the scarless baby root

It takes a forest fire, but I'll turn it all to soot.

May 16, 2017

(If a corpse's heart still beats)

And in the grave it's quiet today,
the ghosts have all flit away,
like he answered my prayers,
and like renewal is a real thing,

like if I get tired enough I'll lay
myself down in that empty hole,

and the vines in the earth have something to say,
they wrap themselves around my wrists, but I'll only
listen when a thorn catches my skin, we always
need a little hole in our veins (it acts as a drain)

and if I fall asleep like this
maybe I'll wake up as someone else
I think she'll look like me
when I was younger

May 24, 2017

(Possession)

When the woman vacated her own premises,
we told her to board up the house because
vagrants could come and make it their own
and we call this repossession or just
Possession, and so when you empty
yourself out make sure to board up
the house

May 24, 2017

(Death of the childhood)

For the good of our whole community I decided that a funeral was the most apt way to
consecrate this ground that I can no longer stand on,
But I do not know who's died yet,

My body bore a weight without telling me,
just as I do not tell my friends when something is wrong with me,
(just as I do not speak of any hole),

it is still reticent
and I do not blame it

It will not list its grievances in a public forum,
but in a confession booth with no one on the other side,
and if a wandering rat hears it he will cry for us both,

and as I finger the rosary beads I will only be muttering to myself,
I will pass every pew as if they were years I hardly remember,
I will not kneel there, I will walk through the open door,
and ask my body for its forgiveness

May 24, 2017

(Hope versus a hole)

Really, there is only one hole (I think, the most futile thing),

But sometimes it feels that I am only this hole and everything gets sucked through it, so that it slips through my fingers, and nothing belongs to me, and death is a reality that I live with, rather than an event far away, because it will happen at one point it is happening now, and I would like to be released from this, but I am pushing a boulder up a gravel hill, and sometimes it feels good to let my feet sink, I no longer want to look for the top of the mountain, I no longer want to be a hole, I no longer 'know' anything at all

But I have written things like this before and I have changed.

March 29, 2017

(Body language)

A slow and steady rhythm, a butterfly
each body is our own, it is the twin to our soul,
(if only we listen, introduce ourselves in kind)

my body once handed me a rope, from which I could climb

my body once knew more than the doctors did, it's true,

my body knew stability before I could sniff it, like a fox in its
hole,

I was quick to stay hidden.

My body knows truth, my mind knows the lies.

I was wrapped up in them like a makeshift disguise.

I can look into my chest and there's a city inside,
whose natives are friendly and whose rivers are wide,

I can fall asleep in this, now,
I can love and desire.

There are things that it calls for,
and these things are now mine.

(there is nowhere to hide)

May 30, 2017

(Murderous)

I have been sitting cross-legged under a sea that falls from the sky,
like a curtain of water that won't touch the floor, I've been
picking out seashells that float down its river, looking for
clues, for something I'd remember, I say I'll burn all of
knowledge if it means I'll be safe, a thousand page book
that really says nothing, I'm discussing the sources but
it does me no good. It feels good to talk, but let us not
pretend, there's any way of knowing, how this all began.

There's really no way of knowing, and there's nothing to know.

I dig myself down into a safe and homey hole.

I sit here for awhile, like a well planted seed.

I used to think myself evil, like my thoughts betrayed me.

There is really nothing to know, and I am suspicious of what I can feel.

Neither closes the loop.

Neither lets me be real.

Let me stay down here, for awhile,
overnight, train to nowhere, train to your ready side.

I am ready, too, honey,
I am ready to die.

May 31, 2017

(Caramel)

I have a number of grimoires and each is the
perfume of my evering eruption and so
if I say I'm healing oh I'm healing and
if I say today is new then it is virgin and
if I decide to be happy there is only the gold
that I once spoke of, that I dreamt of, that I heard
of, in a vision delivered to me by that solid angel,
so reliable, if I dial him up. I am delivered to the
eternal, oh, no, that stresses me out, today I am
Wednesday, tonight it is us, I'll wear a caramel
perfume, I've decided to trust.

May 31, 2017

(Waiting for you to ring)

I am in heaven's envelope, I am breathing the cherry fumes,
I am a child from my own womb,

Water dripping in a Turkish bath
(at the same time he strikes the match)

I am opening the door, belly out,
red on my heart, fresh face feeling,
blind woman touching my fingers
to the blue of your shirt, saying,
"is that you?" and giggling like
a candy-coated girl, youth is my
secret, the thing that sustains,
and unfolds in maturation,
goat on its mountain,
flame rolling in the vestibule
down below, oh, oh, oh, it
feels like an itch, but it's a
flower, and in each and every
hour, I am but yours.

If I kiss you
it's to reveal a fraction of the times that we are welded,
and if I'm going to be candid,
I'd wear any ring that you choose.

May 31, 2017

(**Paris in June**)

June is a beetle that I like, one that crosses my arms
as I lie in the transparent bath, oh, transparency, a magic
trick I once dreamt up, thin skin, honest bones, I promised
to show you all of my soul, it has its own highway, from one
galaxy to ours, every morning I call to it, and a little more
seeps out, and I present it on a plate, and maybe you can't
smell it, but it sees you, we both can nod.

Paris is a city I think of, that I lived in a June long ago,
a July, an August, a summer in a city after the turmoil
of breaking from the turmoil itself. Paris is something
I return to. You call me American but the soul remembers
other things. Like Marie Rose Petit, my eighth great
grandmother. Born in Paris in 1646, the bones know
of these things. I know of these things. It is a galaxy,
too, ancestry, you carved my bones.

June is a gift from the gods. And so if you see me change,
before your eyes, know it is a divine transfiguration, just
as the body turns to bread, mine turns to wine, the kind
that I glut myself on, a dream, a fantasy, a truth. The soul
becomes stable, like the walls of a home, one that I longed
for, one that you built with me, ever so slowly, we wipe the
sweat from our brow and lay beneath it.

When I sleep with you I dream of you, and when I wake,
I put my fingers to your face, and breathe your name in
soft resignation (June delivered me of my dreams and
planted me firmly on my feet. The siren, she calls to me,
but I cannot hear her through the threaded gold, I will
love you until we're old, and I will remember last June,
when we loved like children, shyly, like Paris was in my
veins, still).

June 1, 2017

(Ouroboros no more)

A ram grabbed me by the hand and forced my fingers back,
it bit into my neck until I bled, and I enjoyed it,
I tied my toes with strands of grass and said, yes, I am here,
on earth like the rest, ah, the pitfalls of feeling.

Twisted up and reading.

I think it is always like a flash flood on the inside,
with all our hard-earned belongings floating down
the dirty water. Oh, I am on the floor.

How much of my soul is on the top shelf,
waiting?

It can only laugh at the hysterical
histoires, like a woman on drugs,
that's what I am. Deranged.

Lunatic eating her own skin,
saying, this is how I'm born again.

Though it isn't through destruction that we learn to create,
it is through creation, stupid.

The snake lays its eggs.

June 2, 2017

(Capricorn rising)

I have such a small body
it's hard to admit to its
inherent latent power

Two limbs like willow wisps
Two limbs like thin haunches
those of a faun

Women that are born of the
ancient horned one

I seem to dance around it
because I am the
nymph, too

And so if I wake up one blessed morning
with my limbs buried in moss, and my head
hurting with the burgeoning of horns,
please let me run off into the forest

I will return,
more solid than before

(though this power is of the stars,
it will forgive the land, and imbue
it with war)

For I am red, too,
and hurting for more

June 2, 2017

(Behold: I am melted gold)

I am thoughtful, the motion half of undulating,
the mental ocean, the commotion dies down to
a murmur. And it dances like the summer, and
I desire promises, golden perfume, fondle this,
stretched out in fragrances, rouged pink and
caresses,

a mountain of peace.

A moment, I holler,
I swing from one branch
to another,

I am kissing you
in two hours,

And you bathe in me,
heaven's fragrant showers,

I have been waiting to be born.

A dedication to what can only unfold,
(it is too much, that heated beating roar,
I will marry it until it holds me down
and fucks me to the floor)

June 2, 2017

(Tiny little moans)

Curses through me it
courses through me it
lobbies for more space
in my veins and stretches
them apart saying here, we've
made a space for it, here, and it
is underground, now, a dying
rumble, hell's orgiastic grumble,

it is something I could not find in the books,
those reductive delineations, it is something
I found in a painting, and that hit my heart
like Cupid's arrow, it seeps from my marrow
and I like it very much.

I sit at its table, round wooden, supple,
and the king that has reigned over me
for twenty-one hundred centuries puts
down his fist, and tells me: it's going to
go like this. And I listen, and nod, my
knees all atremble, and his eyes burn
me into rubble, a desecrated home,
the youngest daughter, taken for
the throne. Pillaged till I'm perfect.
A hundred tiny moans.

(That collapse into one. This is living,
and re-rendering, the sap of our naked bones.)

I let him bite my wrist, he sucks until
I come.

June 2, 2017

(Breath)

Humidity and liquidity,
fogs that haven't let me go,
You are the clearest person
I know. And you pull me from
the water and you kiss my gills
away, I wasn't born to be a dweller
of the river or the bay. I'll happily
sit beside it, dip a toe in now and then,
but with you here beside me, there's no
more going in.

I'm awake by the fire. And you hold my hand.
It takes a moment to dry off when you've never
been on land.

June 3, 2017

(Gold, purple, green)

Could it be that I'm golden, too?

That I am worthy?

If worthiness is pain I know not how to pursue it,
and I wouldn't, but if it's what I feel it to be,
a surrender to the truths we can't escape,
then yes, maybe I am worthy and worthiness
becomes me like a slow-ripening fruit.

If worthiness becomes me
maybe it's been in me all along,
and I am but the lizard growing
its tail, after having it severed off.

I am happy in knowing this,
Peace becomes me, too.

June 4, 2017

(As if there's more to say)

I moved my plants outside and I moved myself to a mountain,
where I could scream from the tops and nobody would hear me
and that way when I came back down I wasn't afraid of whispering
even if it was the truth that I whispered to you, into your ear and you
would just keep talking because none of it's surprising, I was known
all along. No use in hiding.

I sat in the bath and thought to myself that the costumes are okay but
I must do away with the masks. There's nothing wrong with embellishment
or imagination (it helps us grow) but when it comes to disguises I need them
no more. And you will see my plain skin but you won't blink an eye, because
you've seen it already even when I thought I could hide. You can see me, you
can see me, you can see me more than me sometimes.

June 4, 2017

(Soil)

Kisses from the verge,
I think I'd like to pull you under,
As my tail quivers around the molten core,
and my fingers reach for you, deftly, and my
eyes widen, carefully, trying to see if you see
me, and if you can understand, the depths of
my very being, I cry when our kites fly by two
feet apart, never entangling, I cry at being in
the air at all.

I'm from an earth somewhere far off,
whose soil is moist with the heavenly
secretions, and whose inhabitants
are what here we'd call creatures,
who feed off of a steady diet of
pleasure and honest loving.

I think you could understand that,
I think - and when I fall asleep into
my own becoming, I think it doesn't
matter either way.

I will be red and black,
either way.

We will love,
either way.

I will seep into the soil,
and reach for you,
either way.

June 7, 2017

Violence

(Hell had a child)

I wear Lilith's perfume,
and claim her as my foremother,
just as I say to myself "I am the lightest
and youngest princess from the darkest
and oldest kingdom."

I dance with an
herbal incense to music sung in a
language I could never learn to
speak, though I tried, as a child,

I dance as the Luna but the Luna
that has slept for a thousand years,
I am not sure if it's your kiss that will
save me or something else, my own
prying claws ripping my body in
half.

Really, I would like to laugh,
the laugh of a lascivious woman,
whose cheeks stay rosy all day,
I would like to live as she does,
like the whore, like the babe.

And I say: we must learn to evade
any and all sense of shame, though
it plays a part in my erotic games,
though it is a barbed wire, tearing
apart my slight frame. Though it
keeps my cheeks rosy, and calls
me depraved.

(The word like a crown, but underneath,
I am more loving).

June 7, 2017

(Sight)

If the sky is blue today (a Thursday)
just as it was blue everyday I walked
through the snow, in St. Petersburg,
to the blue cathedral of my school,
if it is still blue today, then let me
have truths.

I must confess something:

I am one of the Fates, but I
buried my eyes in the dirt, on a dark morning,
behind the house, on a hill. I buried them deep
and couldn't even cry for it. I - I pretended to be
blind.

And so when I stared up at the sky in St. Petersburg,
I would tell myself it was the same sky as California.
And I would meditate each day, without knowing
why.

The snow melted and my eyes were pushed up
by a spring sprout. And so what am I to do?

When I play in the yard I sense them, watching me.

After the sun has fallen, I will go back into that yard,
and claw them from the ground. And place them in my
mouth, and swallow each whole.

Round little globes,
a woman knows.

Even when she hides it.

June 8, 2017

(Tired violence)

Tired violence

What lives in me feels incomplete,
a wet breath living behind a curtain.

Vampire I'd invite in, for it's pleasant.

Anger at the world, shuddering, fists
that want to break the surface, muttering,
This isn't me, no, it's violence, my other name.

Violence that plunged me into darkness,
the kind that I'd lick up, my flesh looking
pale in contrast, my flesh looking pure
in contrast, my hair long and feral.

And purity's a flame,
and I'm cleansed by its
renewal, I have been here
before, now I must admit to
being cruel,

and maybe that will tame it,
the surrender to its likeness,
I no longer want to fight this,
I am my shadow, too.

June 9, 2017

(Labyrinth)

What keeps me from clarity? Oh,
shadow girl, whose tentacles grow in
the grey of the pool, I am weaving my
own webs. In secret, always in secret,
subterfuge, clandestine, I will find
my own way through the forest.

(Without you)

My secrets gather dew,
and every sprout is borne of them,
and every truth is first known by them,
and every time I tell you something, I've
given it a good looking over, dunked it in
water, preserved it until it flowers, and then
it can see the light (our light, our summertime
home, I want to be known, I am trying).

(With you)

Pry my mouth open and leave it that way overnight.
We'll see what crawls out, the insects that found a
home in a windowless room, and what else? The
truth?

I know who I am,
I don't know how to tell it.

(Underground communication, my hand reaches for your arm,
what could my fingerprints imprint on you, my skin screams
my secrets, my mouth remains open, silent)

June 9, 2017

(Repairs)

If I kiss you and say "Forgive me for all my misgivings,"
would you know it? Each tiny crack in the pavement
can disappear overnight, if I wish it, and every tear
in my heart can be forgotten, until the angel cells
repair it, they do this every night. They only thought
that I didn't want them to complete the project, thought
I was digging my own fingers into the gaps, every night.
I drew up the blueprints, the forecast and futures, and
I said: "each of these lines will have to be paved over.
Please, start today, do the work that should have been
done last year, do it now, wipe my tears. The divine leak,
even that, can be patched up."

We will not dam it, we'll reach a hand in, and understand it,
stare into its pools, and dismantle it. We are not a leaky heart,
leaving a foot of water to tread in. I announce this now: to all
shareholders with interest. The hole will be patched up. I now
can promise this.

The hole will be patched up,
the hole will be patched up,
the hole will be patched up,

- the headline of every major news outlet.

Screaming from the rooftops, I no longer want this.

A divine lamentation, convalescence.

Repairs begin tonight.

June 9, 2017

Part II

(Out of a dream)

The snake slivered out of me,
there is no use in denying me,
it said so plainly, there is no use
denying your skin. And the faint
shadows of scales that cover it,
there is no use in trying.

Keep the secret to yourself,
but let it flower,

Slither, girl,
be a girl,

be what you have wanted to be.

(We've already divined your destiny,
though it still uncoils every moon at your feet,
soon it will be the only thing that you see,
soon there will be no more trying.)

June 10, 2017

(Seismic shifts)

Pangea rests easy while
one part of her heart drifts
away, a land that came from
the ocean and deserves to be
submerged once more. Primal
screaming, that of a child, who
now is healed, and can go back
to sleep. It seems I always am
shifting, collapsing and re-
building, repairing and re-
paving, or moving far away.

I don't need a new house for this
(I've lived in seventeen, the earth
won't stop shifting below my feet),
I can stay where I am, build where
I am, be where I am, let the shifts
rearrange me, until I am a home.

(My body is a home, my heart is a
home, I am an empire all aglow,
reunited with its empress.)

(The shifting created a doorway,
once I entered, it could close.)

June 10, 2017

(Purity's a rose)

purity's a rose, and I'm flowering,
I'm rewriting the story I started long ago.

When I was more innocent, didn't look it, though.

The sun light covering the slopes of a field,
the cows grazing, the woman, bathing,
two lovers holding hands and walking.

I'm full of ideas, and I'm talking,

purity's a rose, and I'm flowering.

June 11, 2017

(Fire and water)

Saloma sways inside me, a
column of water, undulating.

The mind seeks a haven.

The garden of my flesh.

ANIMA, I have carved the body out,

my skin will hold you,
hugging your sides,
you are my sides,
my rivers.

The fire that burns me is my own.

Teach me how to sway, I am not afraid,
any longer.

I kept the promise.
(I moaned the dream).

June 12, 2017

Violence

(Fire and earth)

He sits in the castle and waits for me,
princess, wobbling knees,
He sits in the castle and cradles me,
father of all the land,
his is the hand that holds my hand
and leads me through the fire.

(animus...) I whisper in a room only lit by a candle,
he, too, lays waiting in the dark, and I am ashamed,
at locking him away, I'm sorry, oh father. Oh king!
the one that desecrates me. My left hand.

The castle, the fortress, the walls protecting me
(and my heart). The legacy, our covenant! Oh
emperor, I cannot rule alone.

Oh, fire,

light me up.
We are together.

June 12, 2017

(Snake girl, woman)

I'm a snake girl!
A burgeoning snake woman!
I am curled at the feet of my own
(everyday, slowly) realizing, I am
a seed that must sprout, as it's spring
only for one more week, I have the idea
but not the strength to be it, what holds
me back? A tarp sack, I've been kidnapped
by my own past - oh, I'm escaping! No more
empathy for the reasons to hold back. I think
it takes some dancing, I think it takes some
admitting, I think it takes some time.

I'm a snake girl,
slithering through my own yard,
hoping the passerby's will notice,
and exclaim at my shining black
scales. I think I like to shock, I think
I always have. Snake woman in the
circus, blowing out fire. The crowd
gasps, covers the children's eyes.

I'm a snake woman,
who dreamt of snake tattoos,
red and black, down my back,
a true admission. I'm always
reminded of my mission, and so
why do I procrastinate it? Is it
incredulity, discouragement,
old-fashion self-punishment,
or a lack of faith? I am the
snake woman, praying on
my knees.

Faithful to this thing in me.

June 14, 2017

(Uranus)

I dreamt that I protected a grub,
a little sliming worm, he walked
slowly, I had to help him keep up.
He'd nuzzle his head between my
legs, he was moist and soft.

I knew he'd grow into a man, if only
I helped him walk.

I dreamt that Uranus is darker than
I supposed, clandestine experiments
conducted in underground shadows.
I dreamt it had more water than I
thought.

I awoke and grew angry at the emptiness,
the sun's light revealing all my laziness,
my inertia. The sun's light, it melts my
bones, still chilled from the New York
snow,

Moist and soft,

I have more water than I thought,
thick black water,
darkness and rot.

June 15, 2017

(I'm going to stay)

I know Goodbye.
I've done Goodbye a number of times,
I know the resurrection that comes with it,
the flames.

I know how I grasp onto myself,
re-align,

Solitude as a remedy,
solitude as self-love.

I want to be the flames, here,
in our cave.

I want to learn "I'm going to stay."

June 19, 2017

(Great expanse)

My brain is so big I can sit in it

I got lost in it, for some number of years

Not tunnels, but a great expanse of space
whose weathers are controlled by the heart

I got lost in it, for some years

(until the heart could not reach me)

Let alone a body,
I had longed to know

I got lost in a mind,
lost in images,
lost in weather

I was lost to a heart
that slowly did wither

I was lost to it

I was lost

At the end of the great expanse of space was a field
(was a heart) and at the end of its river was the wet-
ness, was the cleft between two legs, was my pussy.

June 20, 2017

Part III

(Beast/basement/debasement)

Oh Romance,
oh, Violence,
oh, woman crouching behind the curtain,
long dark tongue, stained with blackberries,
oh woman, beast, primal little thing, you are
collared in gold by the queen of this abode,
she calls you her princess, she leaves your
hair uncombed. Oh Violence, oh Priestess,
your heart beats louder than a drum beats,
I heard you came from the jungle, is it true?
Is it real? Is your tail hidden between two
legs, are you real? And are you mad? For
when the queen feeds you fruits, and
provides you with a bed, your wildness
seems to temper, but your appetite's not
whet. What do you long for? What do you
desire? What do you dream of? when to your
little bed, you retire-

oh, monster,
oh, writhing,

I find you in the morning,
sleepless and still tired.

Hungry and on fire!

I find you in the basement,
crouching and licking spilt water.

June 22, 2017

(Fuchsia lipstick)

I still look young.

The woman with the fur boa, satin gloves, satin gown,
red carpet, glitter eyes, painted mouth.

(secret courtesan, wealth on her fingers, a locked away gun)

"I gave him two options. I said, you can either have me, or let me go free,
but let me tell you, I think you'd regret it, I think you'd regret it, I think
you'd regret-"

Coral lipstick fuchsia lipstick blood-red lipstick purple lipstick

"I told him, I'd get in that car and drive off into the sunset, but I think you'd
regret it, I think you'd regret it, I think you'd regret it,"

I got my nails done, pointed but not sharp,

"I think you'd regret it, I think you'd regret it, I think you'd-"

I fell asleep beside him, silk robe, feathered mules.

"He told me to stay and I kissed him. I never had a car, anyway."

I still love him, to this day.

June 22, 2017

(Fuchsia lipstick pt. 2)

She always signed her letters with a fuchsia kiss. I pressed my lips against it in the dark of my room, only the lamp on, the traffic outside, glorious, every noise, filling us, the space I created, between us. Every letter set me aflame, I became a bottle rocket, burst like three fireworks, above smiling faces.

I wanted her to sign it with "Yours," or "Love," she didn't do that, we had only met once, at summer camp when we were little. She was beautiful then, I'm sure she was beautiful now. I could smell it on the paper - a whiff of her, of her cherry perfume. I asked her to send a photograph, she never did. I could only imagine, the arch of her brows, the length of her hair. A halo around her, always.

We were nearly eighteen when she met a man, moved away, I didn't hear from her ever again. But every woman I passed looked like her, or like what I had imagined her to be, the hair always changing, the lips always rouged, the hips ticking back and forth like the minutes that escaped me, the hours, the days, oh, the years! The years without her.

I imagined that I was a vase, and she my flower, and everyday I'd water us.

The world one field of wild flowers, that I'd pass through, looking for her bud.

She signed each letter with a kiss, I'd kiss her back in the dark.

I smelled her cherry perfume, I smell her now.

June 22, 2017

(Untitled)

I left my man on a rainy day. I went to the fairgrounds, they had just set up shop, I wanted to ride the rides. It was only drizzling and the ferris wheel still spun, slowly, cartwheeling in the sky. I sat alone, I lit a cigarette, my white scarf tied around my face. Big black sunglasses, movie-star style. I puffed and puffed, my red lips leaving a mark around the filter. Something my mom used to do. I let the metal contraption lift me up and then bring me back down, I let it, I let it.

I left the fairgrounds and went to a cafe. Pulled out a notebook, something I'd stuffed in my purse. Had to ask for a pen, the waitress obliged with a strained smile. And I wrote - or, I tried to write. Never really was the type. I sat in the cafe and wanted to write about my life, about my man, about my mom, but nothing came out. Nothing! Not a word, not really, nothing other than "When I was a girl..."

What was there to say? I was never a girl. I was born in these white leather kitten heels, I was. Born in stockings with my nails done all fresh and sharp. Born whining about the television set not working, born burning toast. I had no story.

I was a caterpillar in the womb and a butterfly upon birth.

I came home, I slipped back into bed, in an old lace teddy, the kind of thing he liked.

Muttered something about trying to find myself. "But then I realized I had just left myself in a corner of the medicine cabinet, hidden behind your aftershave and my cold cream."

He rubbed my smooth skin and we fell back asleep, the bed surrounded by a pile of my clothes, the scarf, the stockings, and that little white dress that's always made my backside look sweeter than a cream-pie.

June 22, 2017

(Cobra)

the venom seeps from my lips and coats my skin like a protective shine, melts in the noonday sun and becomes sugar, under your hands, over my mind.

the venom has left me

the sugar still coats me

your hands are still mine

(I can feel the design, the things that I've dreamt of, the body aligns)

June 24, 2017

(Coral lipstick)

I was in a hurry out of the house so I applied my lipstick in the rearview mirror. He had the kids today, I could do whatever I wanted. That's what I told myself.

I didn't go to lunch with friends and I didn't get my nails done, I drove to a park, one I had been to as a teenager. I sat in its meadows and I read.

I got lost in the story of a woman who said what she meant. Every time she spoke a line, my eyes were glued to the page like a voyeur.

I fell asleep in the softening rays and when I awoke, it was dusk.

I went home and spoke my mind. And every time I opened my mouth, I found that I had nothing bitter to say. There was only the love I had never had the gall to express.

Everything glowed orange. I had never been so in love.

June 24, 2017

Violence

(Our covenant)

What I had lost,
the knowledge of two blue doors
leading me back to a paradise that
once stood at the crevice of my body,
What I had lost, is more than just that.

I lost the trailing light of my own damn comet,

in mid-space I floated,
trying to identify in a void.

I went underwater and then I
set myself on fire,

the body did not melt,

I melted everything else,

the body is a soul,
is my soul, not just
a soul's house.

What I had lost is,
presence, that string that
ties us back to the ground,
a string I'd thought I'd found
back when I was twenty. It
trailed behind me down
the labyrinth, I kissed
the bull, we walked
as friends. What I had lost is
promise, the soul's undying
wish. It whispers to you the
craziest things, but you must
do exactly what it bids.

June 25, 2017

(Purple lipstick)

I kissed him before I ran out the door. Left a big old purple ring on his face. Lilacs, lilacs, baby. He called me lilac.

Winked and grabbed my bag. "Make sure to bring a pen," my boss had said. "I'm not stupid," I said.

The actress was making her first public appearance on her world-wide tour. No one knew why she was coming to our little podunk town, maybe because she knew it'd cause a scene. My boss said if I could get an interview with her, he'd pay me double the week's salary. I told him triple and he shook my gloved hand.

I could barely make it through the crowd. My patent pumps stepped on toe after toe until I thought I could see the top of her head. Truly, I hadn't heard of her. But the word around the office was that she was the most beautiful woman on the silver screen. A real fox.

With my notebook in hand and my pen between my teeth, I pushed to the front, elbowing the men snapping their pictures. They all held their mouths open, like thirsty dogs.

And then my mouth opened, too. She looked exactly like me.

June 25, 2017

(Red lipstick)

Our first date went, well, really swell. We locked our pinkies together as he walked me to my door. The vines tried to tickle our heads, take part in the romance wafting from our smiles.

He kissed me, not a long kiss, but long enough that his lips were tinted red. I smiled, he smiled. We said goodnight.

I could barely get my clothes off that night, I was in such a tired daze. I wanted to stay up and think about him, but sleep called to me, and so I let it.

I think I forgot to take my glasses off. The next morning, they were on my pillow.

I never told anyone what I dreamt that night. My friends would ask about the date and I'd say, "Well, it went really swell." They'd look at each other like I was holding something back. We'd all laugh and I'd reassure them I was telling the truth.

They saw it, though, something held between my teeth.

That night I had seen our wedding. Full-fleshed, the whole shebang. I woke up and I knew it wasn't just sweet fancy. I woke up and I knew.

June 25, 2017

(It lives in the woods)

It lives in the woods! she said. She pointed her little finger past my shoulder, I turned to look at the trees, shifting and moving with the flight of black birds.

What? What does? I felt unnerved. I couldn't play off childhood imaginings like the others.

She shook her freckled head. If you do not know it now, it will find you later.

I couldn't fall asleep that night. I wrestled back and forth in my cabin, listening to the whooshing of the wind.

As I drifted into slumber, I heard a knock.

And another, and another, and -

I woke up in the woods, naked, my skin covered in little pieces of moss.

I knew that I was lost.

June 28, 2017

(We had never been to the woods)

We had never been to the woods before. The city had a way of wrapping you around its finger. He suggested we get away for the weekend, and I thought he was right, we needed to get away.

When we went online to rent a cabin, I had an urge to pick the one furthest from the park's entrance. I wanted to get away.

And when the animals began to howl in the night, I would lay in bed, smiling at the ceiling. He slept through it all.

The room smelt like mold but I knew it was decay.

We swam naked in a pond hidden by the shade of the trees. I couldn't stay underneath the water for long without hearing their voices. I did not tell him we weren't alone.

I didn't tell him a thing! The knocks at night weren't acorns on the roof, it was them, looking for me. Go back to sleep honey, go back to sleep.

He kissed me hard in the morning - I kissed back. My legs melted below us, into one long tail.

I kissed him back - did he taste the difference?

June 28, 2017

(We spent our honeymoon in the woods)

We spent our honeymoon in the woods. I didn't really want to, but he insisted. Said it was his favorite place, said it'd be romantic. Well it wasn't. Bugs biting me from the moment we got out of the car. I said, honey, let's just turn around and book a flight to nowhere. He said, honey, we're already nowhere.

I could barely sleep that night. Was biting my nails, getting up to go to the bathroom every thirty minutes. He snored like a bear. At three in the morning I gave up and went to sit on the porch (screened in, thank god). That's when I first heard it.

Yes, it could have been an animal (as if that's not scary enough). But that sound... that screeching. Like something was being eaten alive.

I rushed inside and tried to tell him, he brushed me off, and I spent the rest of the night in the corner nursing a cigarette.

And then I slept.

June 28, 2017

(Her turn)

Special, special, special girl,
smeared lipstick and slept in curls,
special special special girl

I think you've been asleep in a cupboard or a drawer

The soul whispered in your ear long ago,

"one day you'll awaken, when it's your turn to rule."

June 29, 2017

(Oceans away)

When was the split?

When did I leave my body, like an abandoned home?

And have I returned? Or do I just visit,
place my spirit in the cockpit,
saying 'steer! steer!' until it's all nonsense,
my experience, it's divided. Perfection / or
improvement, I'd really like to do this,
make sense of it all (sense of the body,
the heart, the soul! Don't make me leave
anymore. I'm pushed out of my home like
a woman foreclosed.)

I thought it was perfect
until doubt crept in and
I became worthless, algae
on a rock that you will
never see.

Yes, that's how I feel.

(To some algae's putrid but it's beautiful to me)
(But will you ever know it if you won't swim in my sea?)

June 29, 2017

(Remember)

Oh, there is algae over everything.

And I am a flame who is rising through the void,
a traveler on the mountain, only led by a dream,
how many times have I followed the instructions
that my sleeping mind has given me?

Rightness, oh, rightness! Summer holds this all.

The times when I'm most frightened
are the times when I am wrong.

June 29, 2017

(Decimation)

Rage, rage, rage, rage, these letters should be red
and all that kills me should be dead,

I will venture to the top of the mountain only so that my gun will aim from up high,
I will stand above every enemy,

Arrows are for dreaming and bullets are for beseeching,
I crown myself tonight.

June 29, 2017

(Decimated)

Yes I once enjoyed being decimated
because how perfect is it to be torn in two
and to see all of your carefully crafted cities
burnt alive? They were never mine - I've created
whole countries so that there would be one forest
for me to hide in. The rest is a stage, oh yes, I pretend

Too much empathy left me devoid of any integrity

Vampyress is violent, and we have been lying

I am a bedroom covered in blood,

I'm pouring the bleach down the sink.

I will be covered in blood, whimpering,

saying, "I only want horror!" That's my

honesty. I only want fire.

I will be electrocuted in a dungeon far away

(in my forest) and the shackles will feel perfect,

and I will be naked, singing, "Decimate me!

Decimate me! Decimate!"

June 29, 2017

(I let the earth fuck me)

(The ocean that'll choke us) is the one we need to cross,
we sailed all night, ignoring the scurrying of rats, I brought
with me four coffins, one for each soul. But I could not sleep,
I sat at the helm, and tasted the salt.

(The island that would save us) is the one I marked with an X,
saying, I love the ones that live here, but oh, I would not. Saying
I am nice, and kind, and can keep it under control, yes, I love the
ones that live there, but I am under control.

When we first landed I didn't know what to do.
I heard the wolves howling, and I looked back at you.

With a look of reassurance, I touched the sand and ran,
my dress trailed behind me, I remembered who I am,

The jungle has its secret, the unconscious hides from us,
I only found my wholeness by learning how to trust,

I dug a little hole in the dirt, and buried my own beating heart,
I told the island's soul: do with it what you must.

(I let the night overwhelm me) and danced with each rising tree,
the passion overwhelmed us and I wrapped my legs around their trunks.

When I woke they'd all turned into cocks.

I let the earth have me, I let the earth fuck me, I let the earth have its way.

June 29, 2017

(Golden feet)

I already know my way - I must live it, I have two feet on the ground,
golden feet, toes curled into dirt, marvelous things. I sat by a river and
listened to its call, I've been doing it for years, now I know what it's for,
and it's a boat for us both, I will sit and you will paddle, we will both take
our turn, pushing back the water,

Every time that I open this shy and frightened mouth,
a world tumbles out, my world, our world, place your feet
onto its ground. Brown feet, beautiful feet, I love your feet,
I love you! Shyness had me crippled, my arms tied up and
glued. I'll say it to you, I'll say it to you, I will say it all.

I'll open my mouth and I will laugh.
I was a child once, no going back,
we create our happiness here, and
I'll kiss you, reveal to you, and love
you with no fear.

June 2, 2017

Part IV

(My land)

Hope.

A land of hope, in which I settle down,
it felt so close, for so very long,

(I crawled through the hole)

and came out the other side.

There is a land where all things are free,
where creating is something that I do to me,
designing the details in a vision so pure,
I sit by the fireside and watch it all form,

I have known this for so very long.

(The body's enclosed by lines)

and so I let myself be born.

July 2, 2017

(The Final Death)

Maybe my body has died so that we may resurrect it, hand in hand,
together, things I've wanted but was too afraid to murmur, I am
only barely covering the body with dirt, for I know

it and I will rise again

July 6, 2017

(Atheist)

I don't know if there's a God in this world other than my body
other than my breasts my lips my yoni

I don't know if there's a God

July 11, 2017

(At least it's honest)

I am the woman burning on her knees,
without shame,

Shame shame shame shame,

The town watches with shame,
as they burn her alive.

July 12, 2017

(The fields are changing)

I think the satyrs are tiring of their dancing,
going limp beneath the sun that burns tirelessly, sadistically,
I saw one lay his head down on the breast of a nymph,
saying, please, just hold me. I have never let myself be loved.

I saw the nymph rest a finger on his temple, though hesitant,
saying, I have never been a lover before.

July 12, 2017

(A butterfly lies dead or hidden on the floor)

Capturing and strangling but keeping one inch from life,
keeping things behind cages, torturing devices on long long
sticks, keeping a safe distance, but hurting nonetheless, I could
never really confess what lives in the shadows of me, and so how
could I pretend, how could I mend, when broken in two by the limbs,
and oh yes, we'll erase what's in the middle, those things only get us
in trouble. And trouble we are, a woman is a target but she drew the
red circle on her belly and said "hit me here."

That's how it feels, doesn't it,
that's how it feels.

I can hardly imagine a field where shame doesn't follow me,
like the night.

And so when I'm pushed to the floor I'll bear my unused fangs
but we both know I have waited for the floor, my fingers, they
curl in the dirt because they have never touched flesh, no,
this is the only earth I know.

I fell to the floor but I couldn't help but get up,
but for the rest of my life I would walk with my shoulders hunched,
covering those two balls of flesh that others wanted to touch,

"I am not what I am" I would cry but oh, please, let me hitch my skirt up a little,
let me be me.

She would once again trudge towards the cave and let her body capsize,
we can no longer hold the shame, we can only collapse.

July 12, 2017

Violence

(Bob)

He is bloodied on the floor
and I killed him!
but he resurrects every night
and tries to get through my door

last time I jumped out the window
he was a panther, I barely got out

some men are more terrifying than animals
I'm terrified of myself

July 12, 2017

(Happy vampire)

I am a happy vampire, I said,
and that felt right, I am one who was dead
but who no longer is dead and who can smile
and, what, laugh?

Something that trickles in me yes
a lost vitality, blood on the floor that
drips from the ceiling, who's hiding in
the floorboards up above? That man I
killed in the heat of the moment, he
tried to touch me and I screamed!
He covered my mouth.

I decimated him and then sat on a stuffed chair below,
saying, I am only innocent, and he was on death row.

Anyone who crosses me will get what they're owed.

(But I'm not murderous, they are, but I'm not murderous,
they are, touch me and I'll scream! I'll cut off your fingers
because you've been mean.)

I'll sit by the dripping of your blood slowly thickening,
content and licking the lips that stay mine.

July 12, 2017

(No name)

I would call him anything in order to know him,
the Hades of my own soul, who leads from the
shadows and won't let me be born, no, not yet,
not until I call him by name. Not until I jump
into the flames!

Not until I'm wounded.

And then the black tar seeps out,
embarrassing, isn't it, how we're all
liquid inside.

Every fantasy, every dream!
Every axe taken to the pits of me,

Every murder, I murder in secret,
where no one can see it, I get myself
off.

I kiss in the darkness, I'm a body in the darkness,
I bleed out in the darkness, I'm a being with no
name because a name would make me known,

I'm the thing in the forest that fills you with its moans.

And you thought you could tear it all down.

You will be sick with this thing until you let out its groan.

(I see you, I see you, I watch you from outside)

July 13, 2017

(Motel)

Pale-yellow skirted babe drives away in a serial killer's car,
she fawns over him, her perfume fuming around them both,
her shaking fingers in his hair, saying, oh, how I've loved you
from afar.

Me too, babe, me too.

Ruthless killer picks up yellow-skirted babe after watching her for days,
resting his hand on her knee then deciding against it, touch is far too
intimate. Turning the music down, saying, oh, how I've waited for
this moment.

At the motel she takes off her earrings in the bathroom, oh,
what a dream come true, she flashes the teeth he'd like to
rip out, oh, what a dream.

In the bedroom he sets up his instruments, long and sharp,
thinking, this will be the last one.

She wraps her hand around the doorknob, thinking, maybe
he's the one.

July 13, 2017

(Animus)

No force sways me, no, I am only a young girl
sitting in a pool of mud, snaking her finger
through the thick, no, mother, I will not
come in and clean up. I feel better here,
in the mire.

I am alone with my own truth,
every grabbing hand is mine.

Yes we relate to the ones who pillage and rape,
yes, we're ashamed, legs closed tight and mystery pains,
even the mirror seems to lie, it won't cough over the secret
that we have been searching for in the pit of our souls,
asking what does it mean to be disgusted without knowing why?

Male hands male gaze male mind,
there's a seed of destruction that I'm trying to find!

Coo-ing and caw-ing like a nubile mother,
saying, I know where you're hiding, it's time to come out now.

July 13, 2017

(Cave paintings)

The man in me is tired,
he lives at the bottom of a cave
and was forgotten long ago,
his bills are racking up,
he has forgotten friendship,
the man in me is lost.

He began to paint on the walls of the cave but that's not enough.

I thought I could be an emperor but my empire washed away in the sea.

I thought I could live this life as just half of me,

I thought I was only woman.

Now I remember something beyond celestial responsibility,
and I am crumbling.

(Man is remembered and identity is washed away in the sea)

July 15, 2017

Violence

(Unus mundus, or, Lilith wants the dirt)

A blocked tear duct!
What a funny thing, an angel,
crying out in pleasure or in the pain
of losing a skeleton that was not mine,
crumbling, rumbling, orgiastic uncertainty,
I'm falling, I want this, I want to be mine.

I will slit the man's throat and take his spirit,
I followed a trail of blood until I found my
own corpse, and crawled back inside her.

(Just waiting to be zipped up)

and I have time to reflect on my nature,
I am wearing wolf's clothes, I am
bathing in slaughter.

I fall to the floor,
an overused metaphor,
we are trying to descend.

Unus mundus, return me to the dirt.
I am the girl eating flesh.

I am the book of violence,
cursed if you read this, fall,
fall, away.

Or I'll shoot you in half! Two
selves is better than one.

(But what will unite us?
Stitch me up now, please.
And put down your gun.)

July 17, 2017

(Summation)

If you haven't followed the story so far, violence lived in the hole,
desire lived in the hole,
I lived in the hole!

Thank god I'm Pandora, thank god, Thank god I'm Pandora, thank god.

July 17, 2017

Part V

(Young as the sea)

I, as a snake, shed my skin from time to time. This time was painful. I woke up with a trail of nothing coming off my back, I asked my cat, could you peel that off for me? I shudder in the shower, oh, things are coming back. Hauntings! We are all haunted. I called in the priest and he blessed my new kitchen. I called the police and they locked up my bedroom. I kissed my lover, a million times. I sat on the porch without a cigarette, no more cigarettes, only tea. I fell asleep and reported my dreams like a psychic detective. I fell asleep.

I hung a painting you did and a painting I did. I shed off my skin. I let you take part in the pulling apart and you saw me as I'm meant to be seen - real. I'm real for you, you're real for me, I'm real for you, you're real for me. It's really you, it's really me.

In a spiritless house, in a spiritless dream, I've forgotten the things that used to hurt me.

I am older tonight. I'm as young as the sea.

July 18, 2017

(The witch is a woman)

Mark well, my dear,
you are past the age of tears,
we've had enough water to
resurrect the garden, and
you sit inside while the
demons tend to it.

You sit inside.

The house is a womb, you need a womb,
still barely born, queen of each spirit that
roams in your tomb, you are
the woman who admits!

The grand confessor.

The womb undresser!

The witch is a woman, I have no broom, just long legs and two boobs,
and to those that can see, two horns, and two hooves.

July 20, 2017

(Fortress now)

We are each born with a seed (a woman, a jewel),
and although weeds will grow around it until
we forget it, we still feel it, rooted in our bellies.
We still feel it!
Can't really forget it!

As a child I'd imagine myself with glowing eyes,
a psychic, a mute, I wrote on a piece of paper
telling my mother from now on I wouldn't
talk, but she wouldn't allow it. Mouth
forced open, a hand pries me open
while I sleep, jawbreaker, executioner.

Confess ye sins, you are a woman, and so you are obligated.

(Permeable boundaries, men are made of lines, but I am
made of waves, and have never felt closed. Even when I close
the doors to my heart a stab rips them open, I read a book that
said there are no degrees of openness, you're either open or
closed. So which one am I? Always in hiding. Always reminded
of the secrets that hold my throat. Only the devil in the form of
a young girl will rip me open, screaming out my shame, saying,
Lauren, your tolerance is lame, you are one thing, a line.)

My seed or jewel is, well, evil.

I will join the dark ones and be enclosed by lines.

Thank you, fortressed one. For so long I've been looking for a home.

I will bolt the door closed and admit to everything. Everything!

July 20, 2017

(White science vs. black magic, or me vs. me)

Now that the storm, oh storm, has passed,
only the wife and mother stand on the hill, together,
peace I suppose isn't something interesting to write about
it is the thing we're all gunning for, though. Hard to admit
it's always been a possibility, hard to admit the only war
was in myself. And so the rubble and ashes that I expect
to see at my feet are not there, and the scars are all gone,
hallucinating woman, the devil has never known your name.

Every possession film is a story of a woman vying with herself,
slain by herself, desecrated by herself, oh, every grabbing hand
is mine.

Neuroses, floating entities, exorcism or talk therapy,
my confession was to you and then it all flitted away.

I will leave the padded room now, I guess I taped the key to my leg.

We have gone crazy in order to grab onto sanity,
saying this is my birth right.

We have gone crazy because that's what women do,
right?

July 21, 2017

(Silver scream)

Vampire woman who dreamt at night of being a daywalker,
of curling her hair, putting a heeled foot down upon her threshold
on a sunny morning. Vampire woman orchestrated a few auditions,
but after eight, saying yes I will star in your lycanthropy movie, are
the murder scenes at night? Good, I will be there. Yes, I can scream.
A pair of tits, too! Pale enough to see the veins, though they're no
longer there.

She curled her hair, applied a feminine rouge, and she screamed.
Now the people will hear me!

But when they processed the film, she couldn't be seen.

Only that haunting and melodic scream.

Back to the coffin, back to the darkness, back to the night.

(What's the difference between being a freak and invisibility?)

July 21, 2017

(Limbo)

I am given up to my own forgiveness,
I forgive you, Lauren, I once had an
imaginary friend and his name was God
or sometimes Jesus and he ALWAYS forgave me,
I'd walk around in circles and tell him of my sins.
Really, without shame, because we both calculated
the smallness of it all. He loved to listen, and he
understood, because he only saw the world through
my eyes (and everyone else's, when he went to them).

My god was forgiveness. That's something worth believing, no?
That's something worth forgiving, no?

My left arm was forgiveness and my pinky was beauty (Aphrodite)
and in my belly was Lilith and her red spit. I deified every cell
of me, I worshipped myself selfishly.

I can still do that, with no gods.

If I can forgive me, I can finally be free.

(Like a child in limbo, I always imagined it to be like
a womb floating between here and heaven, somewhere
in space. Where there was no bad and there was no good.)

July 24, 2017

(Skinless)

They lowered me into the grave for the final scene.
I lay in a frilled (torn) dress upon someone's coffin,
At peace, total peace, don't you see, what happens
when we give it all up. Sensitive girls are skinless
and yet, covered in ghost skin, each layer a past
we are longing to remember or longing to forget!

I have remembered the better times.

And so I can die knowing life isn't wasted,
and so I can write a story we haven't yet read.

And so I am sated, and so I am fed.

(And so I am yours, and so you are mine).

July 30, 2017

(Oblivion pt. 2)

The hole is much bigger than I,
I think it is much more than a past,
not created by any wound. Or was it?
Am I it? Interiority, I'll dance in my
inferiority, wondering what part I
should cut out. I dreamt these
words: "The void lives in the disconnect
between the body and the mind."

How many books will I have to write until
I'm invited back in? How many loves will
I have to love until I am whole?

How many times will I have to realize this,
until something is united, and I am a functioning
human. And in that moment what dreams will
wash away, until we are but a statue, standing
in the sand.

I can be a solid body with a talking heart,
I can be a stomach of desire and I can have fun,
but for the life of me, I don't know who I am.

And so if there is a void I will let it,
And if I am that void I can't erase it,
And if it's because I am a woman then so be it.

Nothing is as nothing does.
I'm nothing, I'm nothing, I'm torn.

August 6, 2017

www.ingramcontent.com/pod-product-compliance
Lightning Source LLC
LaVergne TN
LVHW011214080426
835508LV00007B/785